From Blank Page to Successful UC PIQs

Strategies to turn your stories into a UC acceptance letter

Rachel A. Winston, Ph.D.
www.collegelizard.com
rwinston@uchicago.edu

Imagine getting your UC acceptance! How? By turning "ordinary" moments into extraordinary stories!

This book offers step-by-step guidance from prompt selection all the way to your final polish, with real examples and actionable exercises.

Hook the readers with engaging introductions, examples, and conclusions so they want to read your essay all the way to the end.

Keep your essay clear while conveying your true self and keeping the arc.

hook → context → action → reflection

You've Got This!

Why Trust Me?

Having served as an essay and personal statement evaluator, reviewing essays for colleges and programs, I know what works and what does not.

Privately, I have walked thousands of students through the chaos and confusion of college admissions, from first-gen applicants unsure where to start, to high-achievers dreaming of top-tier UC and private schools. Some of my students have received full scholarships for college.

As a professor, college advisor, and admissions coach with degrees from UCLA, UT Austin, Harvard, UChicago, Claremont, GWU, and more, I have helped students craft compelling applications and essays that go beyond grades and statistics.

I have also written and published more than forty books on college admission available on Amazon, including my recent book *Winning Strategies for Admission to The University of California* and my best-selling 350-page book for high school students, *Medical School Bound*.

Whether it is cracking the code on UC personal insight questions or navigating waitlists, I have seen what works and built this guide to give you that exact edge.

ISBNs - Paperback 978-1-958558-60-7, E-book 978-1-958558-61-4

LCCN: 2025917507

We work with academic leaders who transform the educational landscape to publish relevant content and advise students of their educational and professional options, with the aim of developing 21st-century learners and leaders. We also work with students to publish their books and present widely diverse ideas to the college/graduate school-bound community. With headquarters in Irvine, California, Lizard Publishing works virtually with authors to edit, publish, and distribute both hard copy and digital books.

This book was published in the U.S.A. Lizard Publishing is a premium quality provider of educational reference, career guidance, and motivational publications/merchandise for global learners, educators, and stakeholders in education.

Book formatting by Obinna Chinemerem Ozuo

Book website: www.collegelizard.com

About the Author

 Dr. Rachel A. Winston is a tireless student advocate. She has served the educational community as a university professor, college advisor, statistician, researcher, author, cryptanalyst, motivational speaker, publishing executive, and lifelong student. As one of the leading experts in college counseling and an award-winning faculty member, Dr. Winston has spent her lifetime learning, teaching, mentoring, and coaching students. Her counseling practice centers around college admissions, college essays, portfolios, and intellectual conversations about life and career pursuits.

She started college at thirteen and graduated from college programs in such widely ranging disciplines as chemistry, mathematics, computers, liberal arts, international relations, negotiation, conflict resolution, peacebuilding, business administration, higher education leadership, interpreting, college counseling, and publishing. Throughout her education, she attended and graduated from Harvard, University of Chicago, University of Texas, GWU, UCLA, Syracuse, CSUF, CSUDH, Pepperdine, Claremont Graduate University, and Gallaudet University.

Her position working in Washington, D.C. on Capitol Hill and with the White House in the 1980s took her to approximately a hundred universities training campaign managers at colleges from Colorado to California, thoroughly dotting the western states. Later, she led college tours with students and their families on road trips throughout the United States. She has taught or counseled thousands of students over her career and speaks at conferences and academic programs throughout the world.

As a professor and avid writer for numerous publications, she won the 2012 McFarland Literary Achievement Award, Bletchley Park Cryptanalyst Award, and numerous other awards, including Faculty Member of the Year, Leadership Tomorrow Leader of the Year, and college service and leadership awards. While studying Human Capital at Claremont Graduate University, she was a scholarship recipient at the Drucker School of Management. She was also elected to the statewide Board of Governors for the Faculty Association for California Community Colleges, where she served on their executive committee.

She also served as a faculty member for the UCLA College Counselor Certificate Program and the Director of Mathematics at Brandman University. She taught at Embry Riddle Aeronautical University, Chapman University, Cal State Fullerton, and a handful of California Community Colleges, including Cerro Coso College where she represented the entire faculty as the Academic Senate President and retired in 2016. Over her career, she taught mathematics on television, in small and large lecture halls, online, and via live interactive satellite and telecourses.

Table of Contents

Chapter 1: Why Your UC Personal Insight Questions Matter More Than You Think 5

Your PIQs could make or break your UC dreams

Chapter 2: Cracking the UC PIQ Code.. 10

Unlocking your mindset and showcase your strengths

Chapter 3: The PIQ Selection Process...13

Finding your golden stories

Chapter 4: Structuring the PIQ 16

Essay structures that hook and hold attention

Chapter 5: Writing With Voice and Authenticity.. 20

Finding your voice and expressing yourself in a sea of possibilities

Chapter 6: Editing Like an Admissions Officer.. 23

Reviewing your PIQ to ensure readability, understandability, and insight

Chapter 7: Different Approaches and Expert Tips 27

Your thinking process and PIQ game plan

Chapter 8: Topics and Models.. 32

Prompt, goal, model, execute, and why it works

Chapter 9: Warning - AI, Authenticity, & Verification.. 48

The University of California's warning to applicants who use AI or provide inaccurate or false information

Chapter 10: The PIQ Workbook...51

Brainstorming and crafting standout UC Personal Insight Questions

Chapter I:
Why Your UC Personal Insight Questions Matter More Than You Think

Your PIQs could make or break your UC dreams

The University of California is a dream destination. However, there is stiff competition and the UCs want more than just grades and scores. They want a well-rounded student who will thrive, contribute, and bring new ideas to their campus.

You just want an edge. You've invested more than half of your life to school and you don't want to be stopped in your tracks. Besides, your journey is just beginning. You need this chance to get a great education and create a life, career, and future of your dreams.

Still, no matter how adept you are at writing, it is crucial to know what the University of California values and how your essays can get you a golden ticket. Your good writing forms the backbone of your Personal Insight Questions and story. Showing "personal insight" and "impact" are entirely different.

Besides, while you have chosen activities that were meaningful to you, questions remain. Will they resonate with the admissions officers? What do they want from you, and how can you showcase your talents and experiences without seeming to be bold, brash, arrogant, self-centered, or some other negative quality? Can you articulate the meaning and impact on you? Ask yourself these questions.

Reflect on the activities you described in your activities section. How do they align with your personal journey? What experiences highlight your growth or resilience? How can you express the significance of these experiences in a way that resonates authentically without coming across as overly self-promotional? You need to strike a balance between confidence, leadership, and humility.

The University of California states in their literature, "don't be afraid to brag". That is a curious statement for the admissions team to proclaim. Bragging is not a highly valued trait and might seem contradictory to what you believe. Besides, essays that boast achievements do not come across as inclusive or sincere. I am not sure that essays sharing why you won, took charge, or are prideful are the first PIQs readers would give their highest ratings. So, what does being self-congratulatory even mean?

When approaching your essays, think about the deeper takeaways or insights behind your experiences. Consider how they have shaped who you are and what you have learned, rather than just listing accomplishments. This reflective approach can provide a more compelling narrative that engages readers without seeming arrogant.

As a former reader of essays on student selection teams, I created this book to share insights into what might catch an evaluator's attention and compel them to select you. The tips you learn will also be valuable for your scholarship applications. It is important to apply for scholarships. Tens of thousands of students every year receive significant money to attend college. And, they are not just perfect students with perfect grades and scores.

So, whether you are a junior getting a jump on the admissions process or a senior who has procrastinated until late November, you are here now. Let's dig in and make this happen!

Picture this.
 It's Thanksgiving and everyone is gathered at the dinner table.
 In the back of your mind, you have essays to write. The application is due in a week.
 You want to stand out but do not know how.
 Your friends share that they are submitting poetic PIQs and unique creative writing masterpieces.
 Your cursor blinks at the top of a blank screen.
 Thanksgiving dinner is calling, but your mind is miles away.
 Your heart races. Your brain is foggy. You wonder…

> *What do I even write that will make them pick me?*

My advice? Start early because this is a nightmare you want to avoid. Here is the truth.

Your UC Personal Insight Questions are one of the most important parts of your application.

Why PIQs Matter More Than You Think

Sure, your GPA is important. Your challenging course load is also a key factor. And, your UC extracurricular activity statements describe what you chose to spend your time doing.

The challenge is that thousands of UC applicants have great grades, killer test scores, and substantive activities. Other students offer geographic, socioeconomic, ethnic, or gender diversity. I know, the UCs are not supposed to admit based on race, sex, color, ethnicity, or national origin though, truth be told, admissions officers highly value diversity and will incorporate this value into their selection process irrespective of the law.

Proposition 209 in brief…

The state shall not discriminate against, or grant preferential treatment to, any individual or group on the basis of race, sex, color, ethnicity, or national origin in the operation of public employment, public education, or public contracting.

Whatever happens socially and politically, at this point, you should only worry about your application and how what you write resonates within the spectrum of prevailing forces.

So, take a deep breath, you cannot control the UCs, but you can clearly articulate who you are and the qualities and attributes you bring. Remember, too, your activity statements are very important. Do not discount these as being trivial. And, of course, the PIQs are the spice you add to your application in an authentic, positive, and expressive way.

So, how does a UC admissions officer decide between two students who look the same on paper? They read your activity statements and PIQs. They learn more about you and what is important to you. You have the chance to say,

"Here's the real me. Here's why I matter. Here's why the University of California should choose me." The PIQs are where you stop being "Applicant #10,492" and start being

the student who built a library in their garage for neighborhood kids.
or the student who learned leadership from inspiring fresh talent into a disbanded marching band program.
or the student who spent summers translating medical instructions for her grandparents.

When done right, your PIQs make the person reading them *root for you*.

What the UC Readers Are Actually Thinking

Let's pull back the curtain for a moment and clarify what UC admissions officers see and think. The readers of your application are not looking for some perfect or a superhuman teenager, even though many students feel that way. Instead, they are looking for someone who will:

- Add value to the campus community.
- Show resilience and initiative.
- Bring a unique perspective or voice.

In January and February, these admissions officers read dozens of essays a day. Seriously.

They are human, just like you. They may start by skimming, focusing form and organization. Then, they delve deeper, potentially becoming captivated by your introduction, bewildered by an overly "creative" approach, or confused by convoluted introductory sentences.

If your opening line is flat and generic, they may continue skim. Remember, they are human. If you had to read thirty student applications, totaling 120 essays in a day, or more than fifteen every hour, you might find yourself skimming after essay number thirty.

Try it. Read one hundred and twenty 350-word essays and tell me what would compel you to read through an essay that is boring or poorly written, even while striving to be fair and equitable to all?

On the other hand, if your opening line grabs their attention, they might just slow down and start imagining you on their campus.

The Story Gap: Why Most Essays Fail

You have probably heard this countless times, but here it is again. SHOW DON"T TELL!

The number one problem with most PIQs is that they tell or present facts instead of show or bring readers into the story. You only get 350 words, the PIQs are NOT like the 650-word Common App essay. With 300 extra words, you can be creative, flowery, and imaginative...not on the PIQs.

Poorly written PIQ:

"I am a hard worker and I always do my best in school."

Better PIQ:

"By the time the cafeteria lights flickered off, I was still sitting at the same table, flipping through a calculus review book determined to raise my grade from a C to an A."

Notice the difference?
One sounds lacks clarity and is vague. The other feels like a real moment in a person's life.

Your goal is to close the "story gap". Take your reader inside a moment to show them how you think and help them understand you better.

A Real-Life Example

Consider *Sara*.

She is a solid student with a UC weighted-capped GPA in the high 3's. She passionately described extracurriculars in her activity section and has a few AP classes. Her goal is to attend UCLA.

When she first started writing her Personal Insight Questions, her responses resembled thousands of other applicants. For example, she wrote,

> *I love science because I like solving problems.*

We worked together to dig deeper into her experiences. It turns out that her passion for science developed after she initially *hated* the subject. She had an embarrassing lab accident and then failed her first chemistry quiz. Ashamed and frustrated, she cried and almost dropped the class. However, Sara met with her teacher during lunch, redid her labs, and even started mini experiments at home. By the end of the year, she had become the top student in her class, tutoring her classmates before school.

Her final PIQ began with this engaging opening,

> *"I nearly quit chemistry the day my hair caught fire on the Bunsen burner. To compound matters, I failed my first quiz. Faced with a choice to seek help, attend tutoring, or abandon the class, I refused to give up. I shifted into high gear, meeting my teacher during lunch each day, and plunging head first into my homework."*

> At the end of the PIQ, she noted that she always pulled her hair back when doing an experiment.

The result? Sara gained admission to UCLA. She may not have had a 4.8 GPA, which is unachievable anyway due to the UC's weighted-capped GPA but her PIQs conveyed a memorable, human story.

The High Stakes

Let's be clear:
The UC system gets over 200,000 applications a year. UCLA alone got 145,058 freshman applications for the 2025-2026 school year. Less than one out of ten were accepted

The average admitted student is not *just* the kid with perfect stats. They are the one whose essays made an admissions officer smile, tear up, or nod in admiration.

Your Big Advantage

If you are reading this, you already have an advantage. Why? Because you are about to learn how to:

- Find the right stories from your life.
- Match them to the prompts that will show you off best.
- Write them in a way that sounds like *you*, not a robot.

This book is not about "faking it" or stuffing in buzzwords. It is all about telling the truth and telling it so well the admissions readers cannot forget you.

The Roadmap Ahead

Here is where we are headed in the next chapters:

1. **Decode the UC PIQ prompts** so you know exactly what they are asking.
2. **Find your golden stories**, even if you think your life is commonplace.
3. **Structure your essays** so they hook the reader from the first sentence.
4. **Write with authenticity** so you sound confident, not cocky.
5. **Edit like an admissions officer** to make every word count.
6. **Study real examples** that worked and learn how to adapt the strategies to your own voice.

Final Thought Before We Dive In

You have a story worth telling, though you believe the focal point may not be dramatic or impressive enough. Admissions officers are not searching for the flashiest influencers or the most well-traveled candidates or those with the most impressive internships. They are equally eager to find the boy who listened to his grandfather's stories the month before he passed away, the family that scrubbed graffiti off the walls of the neighborhood gym, or the girl who read books at the bakery while her mother worked. They want to read about *your* life, told with clarity, reflection, and personality.

Note: The UC PIQs are not like the Common App essay. You can't be as flowery since you don't have 300 extra words to get off track with a theme about climbing a flagpole, describing the shoes in your closet, pretending you are a chess piece, or comparing your business to playing Monopoly. These essays are shorter. You need to focus on telling your stories and providing insights from your experiences.

This book will guide you in sharing your story effectively. By the end of this book, you will have four compelling Personal Insight Questions and four reasons why the University of California will have a hard time saying no to you.

Let's get started.

Chapter 2:
Cracking the UC PIQ Code

Unlocking your mindset and showcase your strengths

You are motivated and ready to start. You are keenly aware that the Personal Insight Questions may be the deciding factor between an e-mail saying, "Congratulations!" or one that reads, "We regret to inform you..." Now, it is time to understand the PIQ process.

The truth is, the UC Personal Insight Questions are not random; they have been thoughtfully designed to give you the opportunity to express yourself in a way that feels authentic to you.

The Eight UC PIQ Prompts

Every UC applicant gets the same eight PIQ prompts. You pick four. For each answer, you get 350 words. No more, no less. Use those words wisely, not frivolously.

1. **Leadership**: Tell us about a time you took initiative or served as a leader.
2. **Creativity**: How have you expressed creativity in your life?
3. **Greatest Talent**: Share your skillset and why it matters.
4. **Educational Barrier/Opportunity**: Share how you overcame an obstacle or took advantage of an opportunity.
5. **Significant Challenge**: What tough situation have you faced, and what did you learn?
6. **Favorite Subject**: Which subject fascinates you, and how have you taken your interest beyond the classroom?
7. **Improving Your School/Community**: How have you made a difference?
8. **Something Else**: What else should the UCs know about you?

What Each Prompt Is Really Asking

Here's the part no one explains. Each prompt is secretly testing a different *quality*.

- **Leadership** = Can you influence others in a positive way, with humility, grace, and impact.
- **Creativity** = Are you a problem-solver, original thinker, or idea-generator?
- **Talent** = Do you have unique skills, depth of commitment, dedication, and perseverance?
- **Opportunity/Barrier** = Do you pursue educational opportunities or rise above challenges?
- **Significant Challenge** = Did you face/overcome problems in your life requiring grit/resilience?
- **Favorite Subject** = Are you intellectually curious? Did a course inspire a research project?
- **Community Betterment** = Do you contribute to something bigger than yourself?
- **Something Else** = What is unforgettable about you that does not fit in the other boxes?

The PIQ Golden Rule: Variety

What is the biggest mistake students make? They pick four prompts that show the similar qualities. For instance, all of them demonstrate leadership in one way or another: athletics, club founder, teaching kids, and organizing community events. While these are excellent examples, what other aspects of your personality can you present to the school? What other skills, abilities, values, or qualities define you or how can you adapt these to show different sides of your character?

Another student might concentrate on problem-solving at home, tackling challenges while rappelling, a love for mathematics, and an accounting internship. These examples, while demonstrating critical thinking skills, need to offer different perspectives, stories, or attributes. What makes you unique?

Think of your four PIQs as a team of superheroes, each with a unique power.

For example:

- PIQ 1: Leadership → Captain Initiative
- PIQ 2: Creativity → Idea Innovator
- PIQ 4: Overcoming a Barrier → Resilience Ranger
- PIQ 7: Helping Community → Change Maker

The goal is for the readers to walk away with a vision of at least four different strengths or attributes you bring to your dorm, classes, clubs, sports, research, or artistic pursuits. Remember, you are applying to a university that values collaboration and how you will fit into their campus community.

A Quick System to Match Your Stories to the Right Prompts

1. **Brain Dump**: Write down every meaningful experience you can remember. Jobs, projects, family responsibilities, competitions, volunteer work, or random impactful moments.
2. **Highlight with Stars**: Put a star next to the tough, harrowing, inspiring, or proud moments where you discovered something new about yourself or revealed insights that transformed the way you think about obstacles, people, school, community, career, or life.
3. **Prompt Match**: Next to each star, write which PIQ prompt that story/moment can answer.
4. **Check for Variety**: Make sure you are not picking four prompts that all point to the same quality. Diversify your skill set while showing impact, humanity, and insights.

Example: You started a peer tutoring group after noticing classmates struggling in chemistry. Possible Prompts:

- PIQ #1 - Leadership (You organized and led the group to discover their abilities.)
- PIQ #3 - Talent/Skill (You used your mastery of chemistry to help others.)
- PIQ #7 - Community Service (You helped others succeed and feel proud of their accomplishments.)

You might pick Leadership or Community Betterment and then use your Talent/Skill prompt for a *different* story.

Common Mistakes When Choosing Prompts

1. **Choosing What You Think the Admissions Committee Wants to Hear:** By manipulating your story to make yourself "look good", your PIQ may appear insincere or fake.
2. **Avoiding Challenges**: Don't be afraid to share your struggles. Showing vulnerability and discussing the lessons you learned can come across as heartfelt and genuine.
3. **Recycling Activities List**: Your PIQs should not simply be expanded versions of your extracurricular activities. While you can and probably will use these activities, the focus should be on highlighting anecdotes from your experiences and incorporating thoughtful insights.
4. **Not Leaving Room for Family Adventures, Unusual Circumstances, Epiphanies from Events, or Fun/Quirky Stories:** The "What Else" prompt is golden if you used effectively.

Case Study: Choosing for Maximum Impact

Meet *Alex*.

Alex was passionate about building robots and competing on his robotics team. He played varsity soccer and volunteered at an animal shelter. As an engineering major, his first instinct was to write all four essays related to robotics: team leadership, talent starting from childhood coding classes, overcoming challenges in robotics competitions, and his interest in physics.

Instead, we built variety:

- Leadership → Training new robotics team members
- Creativity → Designing a custom automated feeding system at the animal shelter
- Talent/Skill → Troubleshooting mechanical and coding problems
- Significant Challenge → Recovering from a torn ACL in soccer

Result? Alex's essays showed him as a leader, problem-solver, resilient athlete, and animal-loving volunteer and not just "the robotics kid." Why? Engineering is about team-building, collaboration, working with others, and overcoming challenges.

Your Action Steps

1. **Download the prompts** from the UC website and read them twice.
2. **Do the Brain Dump** of your top life moments.
3. **Match each moment** to one or two prompts.
4. **Narrow your list down** to four PIQs that give you the widest range of strengths.

Note: If you have the bandwidth, I would write six PIQs and see which ones turn out to be the best. Most people are surprised at how good the ones they did not choose turn out.

Chapter 3:
The PIQ Selection Process

Finding Your Golden Stories

By now, you know which UC PIQ prompts you are considering. However, if you are still staring at that blinking cursor thinking, *"My life isn't interesting enough to write about,"* let's stop that thought right now. Here's the truth…

It is not about having the flashiest story. It is about telling YOUR story well.

Admissions officers do not need to know you cured cancer, climbed Mount Everest, or built an app that went viral. They need to see how you think, how you rebound from challenges, and how you will contribute. And, trust me, your life already has plenty of material.

Step 1: The Story Mining Mindset

Think of your life like a giant hard drive. You have years of "files" with experiences, moments, wins, and setbacks. You lived through the pandemic and probably lived through of life's fires - literal and figurative.

Most students only find the "big" files like championships, awards, and major achievements. But here's the thing. The golden moments often hide in the small, everyday files you thought were unimportant.

A PIQ about the time you taught yourself to cook after your parents started working late might be more powerful than one about winning a debate trophy, making the dance team finals, or earning a big award at school. Remember, you must present your 350-word statement with detail, heart, and insight.

Step 2: The Brain Dump

Grab a notebook. Yes, old-school paper works best here. Write without stopping for 15 minutes. List every single thing you have done, experienced, or learned that felt meaningful, challenging, or defining. No judgment. No editing. If it pops into your head, write it down.

Need ideas to get rolling? Use these categories:

- **School life**: favorite classes, big projects, academic challenges, presentations, art, athletics
- **Family:** responsibilities, traditions, cultural influences, siblings, living with grandparents
- **Passions:** hobbies, skills, talents, performances, music, theatre, fashion, nutrition, fitness
- **Community:** volunteering, activism, helping others, environment, animals, kids, coaching
- **Challenges:** setbacks, failures, losses, death, fires, accident, violence, family drug addiction
- **Moments of change:** times you saw the world differently

Step 3: The "Why It Matters" Test

Once you have your list, circle 8–10 moments that stand out. For each one, ask:

1. What happened?
2. How did I respond?
3. What did I learn and how did it impact my thinking?
4. What are my takeaways or insights?

If you can answer those questions with more than a sentence or two, you might have a golden story.

Sample Event: Learned to ride the bus alone at age thirteen.

Why It Matters: Taught independence, time management, and problem-solving, especially when the bus route changed unexpectedly.

Potential Prompt Match: Overcoming a barrier, leadership, or community betterment if you helped others with the same issue.

Step 4: Small Stories, Big Impact

Some of the most memorable PIQs come from tiny moments.

- **Big Story Approach:** "I led my school's debate team to a national championship."
- **Small Story Approach:** "I still remember the first time my voice shook in front of twenty people during debate tryouts and how that moment sparked a three-year journey to nationals."

See the difference? One lists an achievement. The other lets the reader *feel* the journey.

Step 5: The "Spark Moment" Exercise

This is my favorite way to find stories. Think about moments in your life when something *clicked*. It could be a first, a last, or a turning point:

- The first time you solved a problem you thought was impossible.
- The time you played a losing game and realized what you learned mattered more than the score.
- The turning point when you saw your efforts change someone else's life.
- The traffic accident where the show could not start without you and you found a solution.

Write down at least 5 spark moments. These often become your best openings.

Step 6: Match Your Golden Stories to Prompts

Using your PIQ prompts from Chapter 2, place each golden story under the prompt it fits best. For example:

- **Prompt 1 (Leadership):** Organizing a neighborhood park clean-up.
- **Prompt 2 (Creativity):** Designing costumes for the school play out of recycled materials.
- **Prompt 4 (Opportunity/Barrier):** Learning English while tutoring younger kids.

Step 7: Test for Uniqueness

Ask yourself: *If ten other students wrote about this, would mine stand out? If your story is common, like, "I worked hard in soccer and won the championship," the key is in the details. Add anecdotes, thoughts, and emotions only YOU experienced. Your story or experience may be dramatically different.*

Mini Case Study: Jasmine's "Boring" Story

Jasmine thought her life was boring. She had never traveled far, never won big awards, never started a club. Her brainstorm list included:

- Babysitting her cousins after school.
- Baking bread with her grandmother.
- Taking apart her old laptop to fix it.

Guess which one became her PIQ #2 - Creativity? **The bread.**

"Creativity rose in the kitchen, not the classroom. I remember standing on a stool, my hands dusted white as flour clung to my fingers. I watched my grandmother knead dough with a calm, experienced rhythm. The smell of yeast wafted from the oven, filling the air with anticipation. While we waited, she told me stories about her childhood in Tehran, sharing bread with her siblings, being resourceful, and finding joy in simplicity. Those afternoons lessons taught me patience, precision, and care.

Baking with my grandmother taught me to notice the small details. Too much heat and the bread would burn; too little kneading and the dough would collapse. I loved the balance of art and science, appreciating how careful measurements and timing could transform raw ingredients into something nourishing. That same fascination grew into a passion for chemistry, where I found the same thrill in measuring reagents, observing reactions, and waiting for results. In both baking and science, I learned that patience allows creativity to unfold naturally.

When I think about my grandmother's stories and the warmth of bread pulled from the oven, I realize..."

Action Steps

1. **Do the 15-minute Brain Dump** without filtering your thought process.
2. **Circle 8–10 promising stories** and run the "Why It Matters" test.
3. **Write 5 spark moments** something shifted in your thinking or life.
4. **Match each story to a prompt** and check for variety.

Up Next...

You now have your raw material. In Chapter 4, we will turn these rough gems into essay structures that hook, hold, and wow admissions officers. By the end of the next chapter, you will know exactly how to start, shape, and finish your PIQs so they stand out in the UC reader's pile.

Chapter 4:
Structuring The PIQ

Essay structures that hook and hold attention

Now that you have your golden stories, the next part separates the "so-so" essays from the ones admissions officers talk about in the break room. A great PIQ is not just a pile of good sentences, it is a guided tour through your story, with each stop making the reader care more about you.

Think of your essay as having an introduction, body paragraphs, and a conclusion. If you have 350 words, that means you get three or four paragraphs. Thus, you have either about 116 words in each paragraph for an introduction-body-conclusion or four paragraphs, introduction-Body 1-Body 2-conclusion, about 87 words each. You can choose either, but 350-word PIQs with six to eight paragraphs look very strange, as if you never took an English class or learned about thesis statements.

In this book, I will focus on the two body paragraph type with an introduction and conclusion for clarity. This will give you a solid arc to tell your story and approximately 87 words for each paragraph.

hook → context → action → reflection

Make sure you have a strong introduction. A one- or two-sentence introductory paragraph is not recommended unless you are using a quote or separate power statement.

Some students use AI to craft their essays. This is a definite wrong choice unless you want your application to be rejected. Seriously!

Skip to Chapter 9 for a moment to see what will happen to you if your application is flagged or simply thrown out because it did not pass verification. AI is not the way to go for your essays. They tend to sound inauthentic. Additionally, AI uses common word choices, common syntax, and common structure.

AI also likes six to eight paragraph 350-word PIQs with no thesis statement and zero structure. The PIQ might seem interesting to you, but the structure is very hard for the reader.

This book was designed to help you create a format so you can tell your story in your way with your experiences. Now onto grabbing and keeping the reader's attention.

The 4-Part UC PIQ Structure

Think of your PIQ as a movie. If you hit all four parts below, your essay will flow naturally and keep your reader hooked from word one.

- **Hook** → Grab their attention in the first line.
- **Context** → Set the stage so they understand the situation.
- **Action** → Show what you did.
- **Reflection** → Reveal what it meant and how you have grown.

1. The Hook

Your first sentence is your red carpet moment. The punch or pizzazz you deliver determines whether the reader leans in or leans back. A good hook does one of three things:

- drops us in the middle of the action.
- surprises us with something unexpected.
- paints a vivid image.

Bad Hook:

"I am a hardworking and dedicated student."

Better Hook:

"My literature class started with an essay assignment, although I had only lived in the United States for two weeks and was extremely nervous about writing."

See how the second one makes you curious? You want to know what happened next.

2. The Context

Once you hooked them, quickly set the scene:

- What happened?
- What did you do?
- What were the challenges?

Keep the circumstances tight; about two to four sentences is fine. This is not the place for your whole life story, just enough to make the situation clear.

3. The Action

Here's where you show the problem-solving, leading, creating, and learning. Avoid merely saying you worked hard; describe what happened.

- "I froze, unable to come up with anything. At the end of the grueling twenty minutes, I submitted my blank paper, embarrassed by only writing my name at the top."
- "That night, I vowed to be one of the top students in the class. I practiced writing on random prompts related to our readings until I could easily formulate five-paragraph essays with profound thesis statements."

Specificity makes actions and outcomes believable.

4. The Reflection

This is where most students fall flat and where you can win big. After all, these are "personal insights". In the reflection part you can explain:

- what you learned.
- how you grew.
- how this connects to your future.

Think of it as answering, *"So what?"* Without reflection, your PIQ is just a diary entry.

The Fill-in-the-Blank PIQ Template

Here's a format you can literally plug your story into:

1. **Hook:** "I [unexpected, vivid action]."
2. **Context:** "It started when [brief background of situation]."
3. **Action:** "To tackle this, I [specific actions you took]."
4. **Reflection:** "Through this, I learned [lesson or insight], which I now use to [how you apply it today or in the future]."

Example – Before and After
Before (boring):

"I was in robotics and helped our team win a regional award. It was a lot of work, but I enjoyed working with my friends."

After (using the template):

"The robot's claw would not grip. The mechanical arm kept dropping the tennis ball. Our shot at the finals seemed distant. The malfunction started during the last week before regionals, when my team realized the motor we ordered would not arrive in time. I spent three nights scavenging spare parts from old machines in the workshop, testing dozens of grip designs until one finally held. Through this, I learned that creativity often comes from constraints and that the best solutions sometimes hide in the scrap pile."

Of course, this is not 350-words, but this text offers you some direction in creating your PIQ story.

Tips for Making Each Section Shine

- **Hook:** Test three different opening lines before deciding.
- **Context:** Keep your idea and anecdotes moving with no tangents.
- **Action:** Use active verbs (built, led, designed, created, solved).
- **Reflection:** Connect your growth to the UC values of curiosity, leadership, diversity, collaboration, inclusivity, and service.

Consider your experiences. Look back. What challenges did you overcome? Many of my students seem to forget the details of their challenges since they resolved issues which now seem too insignificant to put in an essay. Events often blur and the only thing that resonates is the outcome: success or failure. Note: your thinking and problem-solving process is often more important than the outcome.

Case Study: From Draft to Done

Draft Hook: "I like helping people."
Final Hook: "The first time I translated a medical form for my grandmother, my hands shook more than hers."

The rest of the essay walks through the situation (Context), the steps the student took to learn medical vocabulary and help others in the community (Action), and ends with how this sparked an interest in public health (Reflection).

Action Steps

1. Pick one of the golden stories your jotted down from Chapter 3.
2. Write just the Hook in three different ways.
3. Fill in the Context, Action, and Reflection.
4. Read it out loud. Does text flow like a story? Does the PIQ sound like you?

Up Next...

Now that you can structure a PIQ like a pro, in Chapter 5 we will focus on Writing With Voice and Authenticity so you sound like a dynamic student worth rooting for and not an over-polished robot or an AI-enhanced storyteller.

This is where we make your essays *pop* with personality and impress the UC readers.

Chapter 5:
Writing With Voice and Authenticity

Finding your voice and expressing yourself in a sea of possibilities

Let's be real. An essay can be perfectly structured and still feel dead on arrival if the story sounds robotic. Big words are not as impressive to UC readers as the language of a teenager telling their story.

Admissions officers read thousands of essays every year. The ones they remember have a voice that sparks their interest and a personality that makes them feel like you are sitting across the table from them telling them your story.

What "Voice" Really Means

Voice is your essay's personality. It is the word choice, rhythm, and emotion that make it *yours*. A strong voice makes your essay:

- Authentic: It sounds like you, not like a generic "college essay" or formatted like a sample essay.
- Memorable: The reader hears *you* in their head.
- Relatable: They connect with you and your personality beyond your achievements.

Why Students Lose Their Voice

1. **Trying to Sound Impressive**: Big words and formal tone kill your personality.
2. **Over-editing by Others**: Too many cooks in the kitchen can strip your voice away.
3. **Copying Examples Too Closely**: You end up sounding like someone else's success story.

The Sweet Spot

You want a balance between professionalism and spunk. You want to show you are serious, while also making the PIQ feel like a conversation. You can think of the PIQ as a smart friend telling a great story, not textbook explaining a concept.

Voice Warm-Up Exercises

1. The Friend Test

I always tell students not to fret. You tell stories to your friends all the time without stressing about word choice. This PIQ process is not that much different. So, tell your story to a friend as if you are describing an engaging event over lunch. Record yourself. Then type exactly what you said. This "natural voice" method is a solid starting point.

2. The "Because" Drill

For every statement you make, add "because…" and finish the sentence. Not that you will write this way on your actual PIQ, but you want to share why and what you learned. This forces you to explain your thoughts and reveal your personality.

Example:

"I joined the gardening club because I love vegetables and my friends and I are going on a vegan diet."

Suddenly, you sound human. You will not write that sentence, but you are beginning to flush out ideas.

3. The "One Word" Challenge

Pick one word that captures the tone you seek: curious, determined, optimistic, sensitive, empathetic, persistent, open-minded, creative, thoughtful, or bold. Then, ensure every sentence supports that vibe.

Before & After: Voice Makeover

Before (stiff):

"Volunteering at the animal shelter was a valuable learning experience that taught me responsibility and compassion."

After (alive):

"By the second week at the shelter, I could clean a kennel, calm a barking husky, and explain the adoption process to those eager to find their special pet."

The second version shows, not tells, and has rhythm. You *feel* the day with them.

The Power of Specifics

Specific details are the easiest way to inject authenticity. Instead of "I worked hard on the project," say:

"I spent two Saturdays in my garage, surrounded by scraps of cardboard and the smell of hot glue, until the prototype finally held together."

Avoid These Voice Killers

- Overusing big words you would never say out loud.
- Starting every sentence the same way ("I did… I learned… I experienced…").
- Hiding behind vague phrases ("It was challenging," "It was fun"). *I don't like the word "it" anyway. Try to replace every "it" with the true meaning. Frankly, "it" makes more sense to you than the reader. I say the same mantra about the word "thing" or a "that". What is a that, thing, something, everything, or anything? For example, "It turned out great. We realized that was the most important thing we accomplished." What do those two sentences even mean? Read your final draft for clarity.*
- Cramming in clichés ("I gave 110%," "It was a once-in-a-lifetime opportunity.").

Mini Case Study: Raul's Soccer Story

Raul's first draft:

"I learned teamwork and perseverance by playing varsity soccer."

His real story? He once played through pouring rain in a playoff game, with mud up to his ankles, helping his team come back from a 2–0 deficit.

Final version:

"By halftime, the field was a swamp. My feet sunk ankle deep in mud and every sprint felt like I was dragging a sandbag. But when I slid through the waterlogged turf to block a shot in the last two minutes, my teammates cheered so loud they drowned out the sound of the rain."

You see him. You *feel* the moment.

Action Steps

1. **Record yourself** telling your story casually.
2. **Highlight the phrases** that sound like you, not a textbook.
3. **Replace vague statements** with specific, sensory details.
4. **Read your draft out loud**. If it does not sound like you, tweak until it does.

Up Next...

Your essays now have structure and voice. In Chapter 6, we will become ruthless editors. You will learn the 3-Question Test every PIQ must pass before you submit, and you will see before-and-after edits that cut fluff, sharpen focus, and boost impact. Our goal is to add compelling insight and impact.

Chapter 6:
Editing Like an Admissions Officer

Reviewing your PIQ to ensure readability, understandability, and insight

You have the structure. You nailed the voice. Now it is time to edit.

Remember, a UC admissions reader does not just read your PIQ, they judge every single word. They may say they do not, but human nature dictates that when we compare two, ten, or a thousand people, we judge. In fact, when I served on some essay review panels, I was actually called a judge. I did not pick the title they called me, but I did evaluate, score, and consider the merits of each essay I read.

Thus, if a part of your text does not earn its place on the page, throw that part out. If a sentence is hard to read, revise the wording. My husband, who has been in three movies, says, "If a moment, interaction, or element in a scene is unnecessary, that part is cut." By paring down the movie or essay, the viewer can focus, reflect, and understand, allowing them to put the pieces, scenario, or story together by the end. The UC PIQ readers need to understand and advocate for you by the time they finish.

One other note that is sad, but true. Since readers are tasked with reviewing and scoring a dozen or more essays an hour, you need to make a power punch in your first paragraph. I have mentioned the importance of the first paragraph before, but now I want to add another piece. Readers will not admit this, but if the first paragraph looks really good and the rest of the essay seems fine, they may skim through, give you a high score, and move on to the next. If thoroughly captivating, they may dig into the meat for curiosity's sake.

A good conclusion is also really helpful. Sometimes, the PIQ is so compelling, readers simply have to read to the very end. However, if the ending falls flat, you may lose valuable points. Now we need to focus on impact, structure, and manageable paragraphs rather than those that are long and convoluted.

So, let's get on to editing!

The 3-Question Test

Before you hit "submit," read each sentence and ask:

1. Does this add new information or insight?
2. Does the writing sound like me?
3. Does each element move the story forward in an interesting way?

If the answer is "no" to any of these, cut that part out. Especially, if you are the type who likes to add lots of details to your storytelling, be careful. On a conversational trip from San Diego to San Francisco, some people wind up in Miami. Thus, if your story is in Miami, turn your pen's vehicle around and head back to San Francisco.

Fluff Killers to Watch Out For

- **Filler Phrases:** "I believe that…," "In my opinion…," "The fact that…"
- **Empty Adjectives:** "very," "really," "extremely"
- **Clichés:** "110%," "once in a lifetime," "I learned the value of hard work"
- **Over-Explaining:** Saying the same thing twice using different words

Before & After Example #1: Trimming for Impact

Before (142 words - not bad, but could be tighter):

"I joined the school newspaper in my sophomore year because I thought it would be a good way to get involved in the school community. I was assigned to write short articles about all of the school's sports games and events. At first, I did not really know how to write about sports and was not on a team, but over time I learned how to interview and good questions to ask. I would spend hours talking to players, coaches, and even fans to get quotes and details. This helped me understand the importance of thorough research. Eventually, I became the sports editor, which meant I was responsible for assigning stories and editing other people's work. Reaching each person and looking up information to make sure it was accurate and interesting was a lot of responsibility, but I really enjoyed the process."

After (67 words):

"When I joined the school newspaper as a sophomore, assigned to cover sports, I immersed myself into the world of reporting. I learned fast, interviewing players and coaches, uncovering details that brought games to life. By my junior year, I was sports editor, assigning stories and sharpening others' work. The role taught me decision-making, collaboration, and time management, but I most enjoyed helping others tell their stories."

In this way, your two body paragraphs can offer stories of impact, showing what you did and how you grew, while the last paragraph, your conclusion, can offer insight. On pacing your essay's word count, note that 350 - 67 = 283. This allows you to have two body paragraphs and a conclusion, each with about 94 words. Remember, your structure. You can use this for the rest of your life, just with additional body paragraphs if the essay is longer.

hook → context → action → reflection

So, what changed between the first version of your introduction and the second?

- Cut weak openers.
- Removed repetition about learning.
- Condensed similar ideas into tighter sentences.

Before & After Example #2: Adding Specifics While Cutting Words

Before (125 words - again, not bad and relatively typical of PIQ writers):

"I volunteered at the local food bank for two years meeting people and helping others. My main job was to work on a food sorting team and distributing boxes of supplies to families. At first, I did not think my effort was a big deal and I needed service hours for school, but over time I realized how much each box of love meant to people. I got to know the regular volunteers who came on Saturday mornings. I also started to understand the challenges faced by the people who received these boxes of fruits, vegetables, and canned food. I learned about the importance of giving back to the community and how even small acts of kindness can make a big difference in someone's life."

After (86 words):

"For two years, I sorted cans and boxed groceries at the local food bank, thinking this opportunity was just another way to log service hours. But the work quickly became personal. I learned which families preferred peanut butter over tuna, who might need an extra bag of rice, and who relied on me to carry boxes to the bus stop. As I exchanged smiles and stories, I became humbled by the resilience of those we served and deeply appreciative of the chance to lighten someone's load."

Note: Since 350/4 is 87.5, we are good structure-wise and have about 88 words for each of two impactful body paragraphs and an insightful last conclusion.

So what changed in this version?

- Reduced the paragraph by almost 40 words.
- Added vivid, specific details (peanut butter, tuna, rice, carrying bags).
- Cut generic phrases ("importance of giving back," "small acts of kindness") that could apply to anyone.

Before & After Example #3: Cutting 62 Words Without Losing the Heart

Before (139 words):

"I joined my school's environmental club because I wanted to make a difference at school and in my surrounding community. Our first big project was to start a recycling program on campus. I helped by designing posters, talking to teachers, and encouraging students to recycle plastic bottles, soda cans, and other items. It was not as easy to get everyone on board as I originally thought, but with an advertising campaign, outreach on the morning announcements, and flyers handed out when students entered the school, we eventually we succeeded. Now recycling bins are in every classroom and we even set them up at local grocery stores. This experience taught me the value of persistence and working together with others toward a common goal. I am proud of the impact we made and hope to continue environmental work in college."

After (77 words):

"When I joined the environmental club, I thought a schoolwide recycling program would be an easy win for sustainability. Instead, I discovered that creating real change meant convincing people using creativity, teamwork, and persistence. I helped design posters, spoke with teachers, and encouraged classmates. After extending our outreach on morning announcements and posting flyers at entrances, we gained momentum. Today, in addition to having recycling bins in every classroom, we created sustainability partnerships at local grocery stores."

Note: Long introductory paragraphs are less effective. Many times students want to throw the kitchen sink into the first paragraph, adding a slew of details that could easily be separated into body paragraphs. Furthermore, it is very hard to read such a long block of words. The easy way to smooth this out is to create your outline first.

Introduction - Hook

Body 1 - Context
Body 2 - Action

Conclusion - Reflection

What changed?

- Removed redundant "why I joined" intro (covered by the action).
- Streamlined the "we succeeded" section into a single tight sentence.
- Made the final sentence punchier and more personal.

Editing Tips from the UC Reader's Chair

- **Trim the runway**: Do not waste your first sentence easing into your story; start mid-action.
- **One idea per sentence**: If you have "and" more than twice, break up the sentence.
- **Swap adjectives for actions**: Instead of "hard working," show what you did.
- **Read backward**: This tricks your brain into catching typos and awkward phrasing.

Your Editing Checklist

1. Cut 10% of your word count without losing meaning.
2. Replace general phrases with specific moments.
3. Kill all filler words and clichés.
4. Make the reflection clear, concise, and connected to your growth.

Up Next...

In the next chapters, we bring this process home with real examples, additional tips, and your PIQ game plan. You will see *successful PIQ topics with commentary*, learn mistakes to avoid, and get a plan to go from draft to "ready to submit."

Chapter 7:
Different Approaches and Expert Tips
Your thinking process and PIQ game plan

By now, you know how to find your golden stories, structure each, write with voice, and edit like a pro. Now, we need to pull the pieces together and see success. Remember, the introductory paragraph needs to have some meat but should not be less than 65 words or more than 135. Body paragraphs need to fill the context and action with interest, intrigue, or substance. The conclusion needs to be a "personal insight". Go for it!

I revised and edited these examples from real student stories, reshaped for this book, and designed to show you exactly how each UC PIQ can be approached for maximum impact.

PIQ 1: Leadership Experience

Prompt: Describe an example of your leadership experience in which you have positively influenced others, helped resolve disputes, or contributed to group efforts over time.

Sample Introductory Paragraph (79 words):

"The marching band was losing members. Arguments over music selection split us into cliques, and competitions felt like battles within, not against, other schools. As drum major, I called a meeting to listen to members, making sure everyone's voice was heard. Each section shared their frustrations. We built a new playlist, mixing everyone's favorites. By season's end, I may have held the baton, but together we won competitions, ate lunch with each other, and created a group YouTube channel."

Why it works: Starts with a problem, shows specific introductory events, ends with a growth-focused idea.

hook → context → action → reflection

Body Paragraphs?

B1 - What was the real problem? Bring some specificity here so the reader cares.

B2 - While you listened to your peers, what did you hear and how did you bring people together?

Conclusion - What insights do you bring about teamwork, collaboration, friendships, and unity?

PIQ 2 – Creativity

Prompt: Every person has a creative side, and it can be expressed in many ways. Describe how you express your creative side.

Sample Introductory Paragraph (76 words):

"When the school play's costume budget ran out, I raided my mom's closet, thrift stores, and recycling bins. A shower curtain became a queen's gown. Soda can tabs became chain belts. The entire cast jumped on board to imagine how to transform their character's clothing into a stunning work of art. On the night of the performance, I smiled as the parents asked me where we 'rented' the costumes, knowing each outfit carried a secret history."

Why it works: Unique visuals, resourcefulness, and a clear creative process.

Body Paragraphs?

B1 - What was your role? Who chipped in to make this happen? What was needed for this play?

B2 - What actions did you take? How were parts sewn together to fit? Curious minds want to know the details.

Conclusion Concept - "With creativity, extravagant, highly crafted materials are not necessary. I discovered that the true reward was in considering possible solutions in a difficult situation and finding unexpected costuming in random discards."

PIQ 3 – Greatest Talent or Skill

Prompt: What would you say is your greatest talent or skill? How have you developed and demonstrated that talent over time?

Sample Introductory Paragraph (85 words):

"I can take anything apart and often do just to see how the mechanism works. Most of the time, I manage to put the item back together even better than before. My first 'patient' was an old blender, but soon I was repairing classmates' laptops and fixing appliances for neighbors. What began as simple curiosity grew into a way to solve real problems and earn a little money. Every screw I tighten reminds me that patience and persistence can breathe new life into broken technology."

Why it works: Concrete action (repair work), evolution of skill, and deeper takeaway.

Body Paragraphs?

B1 - Describe how you started this venture. Were you compelled because you broke a toy, bike, or robot as kid? Did you begin by constantly fiddling with toys? Were you attracted to problem-solving?

B2 - What actions were successful? Which failed? How did they fail?

Conclusion Concept - What did you learn from success and failure? Or, maybe something like this... "Just as I once restored machines, I now apply the same persistence and curiosity to my pursuit of medicine with the goal of helping patients heal and reclaim their life back."

PIQ 4 – Educational Opportunity or Barrier

Prompt: Describe how you have taken advantage of a significant educational opportunity or worked to overcome an educational barrier.

Sample Introductory Paragraph (77 words):

"When my family moved from El Salvador, I spoke almost no English. In middle school, I kept quiet in class, nervously looking around every time someone laughed at me. Then, my science teacher invited me to join the robotics club. At first, I only observed, but soon I was building, coding, and explaining designs in English. My language barrier did not vanish overnight, but with each presentation, I learned that communication starts with connecting to the audience."

Why it works: Clear barrier, specific opportunity, emotional and personal transformation.

Body Paragraphs?

B1 - When did you arrive from El Salvador? Give me context.

B2 - The first time you were laughed at what happened? How about the second? What did you feel?

Conclusion Concept - How did your sense of right and wrong propel you in life. You might conclude with something like…"Robotics gave me technical skills while also giving me a voice."

PIQ 5 – Significant Challenge

Prompt: Describe the most significant challenge you have faced and the steps you have taken to overcome this challenge.

Sample Introductory Paragraph (85 words):

"The summer before my junior year, I tore my ACL. Soccer was my escape, my identity. Now, everything I pursued was gone. Physical therapy became my new training ground. I celebrated bending my knee a few degrees further. I worked out even when hobbling, cheered for teammates from the bench, and led without wearing a jersey. By the time I could run again, I understood that the strength I carried within me could not be measured in scored goals, but in my patience and resilience."

Why it works: Vulnerability, resilience, and redefining identity.

Body Paragraphs?

B1 - Context of the event and your emotional battle.

B2 - What action did you take? What was the mental process you took to overcome your disappointment?

Conclusion Concept - What do injuries, recoveries, and support mean to you now? How do you envision translating this to your future goals?

PIQ 6 – Favorite Academic Subject

Prompt: Think about an academic subject that inspires you. Describe how you have furthered this interest inside and/or outside of the classroom.

Sample Introductory Paragraph (72 words):

> *"History intrigues me by its global story of humanity. After learning about redlining in class, I researched how that action affected housing in my own city. I mapped changes over decades and presented my findings at a community meeting. That night, a city council member asked for a copy of my report. Inspired to continue my research, I realized that history fuels my curiosity and my drive to shape a better future."*

Why it works: Links classroom learning to real-world action, shows initiative and relevance.

Body Paragraphs?

B1 - What city? What problem? What lessons?

B2 - What happened in that community meeting? What were you feeling or thinking? What questions did the audience ask that intrigued you or inspired you to do more research?

Conclusion Concept - Where and how do you envision history to unfold? What lessons will help humanity build a better future?

PIQ 7 – Making Your School or Community Better

Prompt: What have you done to make your school or your community a better place?

Sample Introductory Paragraph (72 words):

> *"When the park near my apartment filled with trash, I stopped waiting for someone else to fix the problem. I made flyers, posted in local group chats, and recruited neighbors for a Saturday cleanup days. Kids came eager to help, painting recycling bins so they were clearly marked. Parents arrived with flowers and planted them around the walkways. The community came together with a resounding commitment I never before would have expected."*

Why it works: Shows initiative, community impact, and personal pride.

Body Paragraphs?

B1 - Give me context into why, the smell, and the consequences.

B2 - What were the challenges in the action you took? Did anything unusual happen?

Conclusion Concept - How does service fit into your life? What does it mean to have a clean and safe community for you and those around you? Maybe something like this. "Now, when I walk past the park, I see green grass and sense the empowered community members who came together to make our park warm and welcoming."

PIQ 8 – Something Else

Prompt: Beyond what you have already shared, what makes you stand out as a strong candidate for admission to the University of California?

Sample Introductory Paragraph (73 words):

> *"Every Friday night, my family makes pupusas. As I mix masa, I think about how my hands move with the same motions my grandmother taught my mother. Tradition, to me, is about carrying forward what matters while making the experience my own. That led me to starting a cooking blog, blending old recipes with new twists, sharing them in both English and Spanish and building bridges between past and future, cultures and communities."*

Why it works: Deeply personal, cultural connection, forward-looking mindset.

Body Paragraphs?

B1 - Context regarding your mother, grandmother, and cooking. Add sights, sounds, smells, and feeling.

B2 - What did it take to create your blog and how did you roll that out?

Conclusion Concept - What insights do you have about diversity, inclusiveness, and sharing ideas with others? How does family, culture, and unity fit into your vision of the future?

Final Tips Before You Submit

- **Read Out Loud:** You will catch awkward phrasing you miss on screen.
- **Get One Trusted Review:** More voices can dilute your own.
- **Check for Variety:** Make sure your four chosen prompts show different strengths.
- **Own Your Story:** No one else can write your story the way you can.

Your 2-Week PIQ Game Plan

Week 1

- Day 1–2: Brain dump and prompt matching (Chapter 3)
- Day 3–4: Write first drafts using the structure template (Chapter 4)
- Day 5–6: Add voice and detail (Chapter 5)
- Day 7: First round of edits (Chapter 6)

Week 2

- Day 8–9: Second draft, tightening sentences
- Day 10: Peer review from one trusted person
- Day 11–12: Final edits and polish
- Day 13: Read all four out loud; check flow and variety
- Day 14: Submit with confidence

Chapter 8:
Topics and Models

Prompt, goal, model, execute, and why it works

PIQ #1 – Leadership Experience Prompt: Describe an example of your leadership experience in which you have positively influenced others, helped resolve disputes, or contributed to group efforts over time.

UC's Real Goal - The University of California wants to understand how you take initiative, motivate others, and create solutions that have a lasting impact. They are less concerned with titles and more interested in how you influence people, resolve problems, and build cooperation. Strong responses show that you can recognize a challenge, bring people together, and guide a group toward a shared goal.

Model Essay - 347 words

When the city announced new recycling rules, my apartment complex was left confused and divided. Some residents worried about fines, others complained about extra work, and many were unsure about which items could be recycled. As president of our youth council, I saw an opportunity to turn uncertainty into cooperation. My leadership role was to make the rules clear, bring neighbors together, and create a plan everyone could follow.

I began by attending the city's information session, where I was the only teenager in the room, and took thorough notes. I organized a bilingual workshop in our community room, using English and Spanish so everyone could participate. At first, only a few people attended, but when I added snacks and raffled reusable bags, attendance doubled. To make the learning interactive, I created a "mystery bin" game in which teams sorted items into the correct recycling categories. Laughter replaced frustration, and participation increased.

Within weeks, I saw results. Complaints decreased, bins were cleaner, and a neighbor told me she finally felt confident about recycling. Almost everyone I knew started getting involved and supporting each other in the effort. They even described recycling as fun. To further inspire those who were not yet on board, I designed a one-page visual guide, laminated the page, and posted one near every dumpster. The city council noticed and shared my guide on their official website, multiplying the impact beyond our building. Our community's recycling compliance improved, and so did our sense of teamwork.

This experience proved that leadership is not about titles but about creating accessible solutions that encourage participation. By supporting neighbors in Spanish and English, I ensured that no one felt excluded, which built trust and cooperation. However, one neighbor replicated the poster in Arabic and another in Mandarin. Now, when a problem arises, whether it involves conserving water or improving park safety, I know how to listen, adapt, and act so that everyone feels part of the solution. I realized that leadership, at its core, is the ability to connect people with each other and with a shared goal.

Why This Works

- **Strong Hook:** Opens with a real problem the reader can visualize
- **Clear Thesis:** States the leadership goal at the end of the first paragraph
- **Specific Actions:** Describes concrete steps with clear details
- **Measurable Impact:** Shows before-and-after changes in the community
- **Thoughtful Reflection**: Restates the thesis and explains broader leadership philosophy

Brainstorming Questions

1. When have you stepped in to guide a group toward a goal?
2. What problem or conflict did you help resolve?
3. How did you motivate or encourage people to participate?
4. What specific strategies or activities did you use?
5. What measurable changes resulted from your actions?
6. What did you learn about leadership from this experience?
7. How will you use these skills in the future?

Skeleton Template

Paragraph 1: Hook, Context, Thesis - Begin with a specific challenge that required leadership. Provide brief background and state your thesis: your leadership role and goal.

Paragraph 2: Actions - Describe the steps you took to address the challenge. Include specific actions and examples.

Paragraph 3: Results - Explain the changes or results that came from your actions. Include measurable or visible improvements.

Paragraph 4: Reflection - Restate your thesis in new words. Share what you learned and how you will use these skills in the future.

PIQ #2 – Creativity Prompt: Every person has a creative side, and it can be expressed in many ways. Describe how you express your creative side.

UC's Real Goal - The University of California wants to see how you generate new ideas, approach challenges in original ways, and turn those ideas into real outcomes. They are looking for creativity applied to solve problems, create opportunities, or make something better. A strong essay will focus on the process as well as the results, showing resourcefulness, adaptability, and the ability to innovate.

Model Essay - 347 words

When my friend broke his wrist, everyday tasks suddenly became challenges, including holding a pencil or a fork. He managed and adapted but I felt compelled to help. Watching him struggle challenged me to find a solution to his problem. Besides, that broken wrist could have been mine and one day I might have a similar injury. I set a goal to design a solution that would help him grip objects more easily while his wrist healed.

I began by researching adaptive tools online and sketching out ideas. Using our school's 3D printer and programming skills I learned previously, I created several prototypes of a custom hand grip that could hold different objects, from pens to utensils. The first version was too stiff, so I adjusted the design with flexible joints. I tested each prototype with my friend, gathered his feedback, and made improvements. Eventually, I found the right balance of comfort, durability, and function.

The final design allowed him to eat and write with far less frustration. His smile the first time he signed his name again told me more than any grade could. Encouraged, I shared the design file on a free online platform for adaptive tools where others could download and print the code and specifications. A week later, I received a message from a student in another state telling me that my design helped her father who had arthritis. My small idea reached beyond my school and into someone else's daily life.

This project confirmed my belief that creativity is the ability to see a need and design a solution that works for real people. The concept required testing, failing, and trying again a few times until the result truly met the need. Now, when I think about creativity, I do not limit my instincts and abilities to the arts. I see my thought process as a problem-solving mindset that could potentially improve lives. Whether I am designing in a lab or brainstorming for a group project, I bring that same approach: look closely, think differently, and build something that makes a difference.

Why This Works

- **Clear Hook:** Starts with a real-life challenge
- **Thesis Placement:** States creative goal at the end of the first paragraph
- **Detailed Process:** Describes research, design, and testing
- **Impact Beyond Self:** Shows benefits for others in multiple locations
- **Reflection:** Defines creativity as problem-solving and applies it to the future

Brainstorming Questions

1. What is the most original solution you have created for a problem?
2. How do you usually approach a challenge that does not have an obvious answer?
3. What tools, resources, or skills do you use in your creative process?
4. Have your creative ideas helped others in a tangible way?
5. What mistakes or setbacks did you face, and how did you overcome them?
6. How has this creative work shaped the way you think now?
7. In what ways will you apply this creativity in the future?

Skeleton Template

Paragraph 1: Hook, Context, Thesis - Open with a specific problem you solved in a creative way. Provide a brief background and state your thesis: your creative goal.

Paragraph 2: Process - Describe your step-by-step creative process. Show how you explored, tested, and improved your idea.

Paragraph 3: Results - Explain the impact of your creative work. Include concrete outcomes and who benefited.

Paragraph 4: Reflection - Restate your thesis in new words. Reflect on what creativity means to you now and how you will use your innovative approaches moving forward.

PIQ #3 – Greatest Talent or Skill Prompt: What would you say is your greatest talent or skill? How have you developed and demonstrated that talent over time?

UC's Real Goal - The University of California wants to learn about a talent or skill that makes you unique and how you have used it to benefit others. They are looking for evidence of growth, dedication, and application. A strong response will show the development of the talent over time and its positive impact.

Model Essay - 331 words

I first discovered my talent for arranging music when our school's small jazz band lost several members and needed a way to perform with fewer instruments. The challenge was to keep the sound full and balanced even with a smaller group. I brainstormed options to enhance our music so people experienced the sound's intent. My ability to hear harmonies and rewrite parts so they fit new combinations of instruments became an essential skill for the band's success.

I began by studying professional arrangements and breaking them down into melody, harmony, and rhythm. Using music notation software, I rewrote several songs so that our saxophone section could carry both melody and harmony lines, while the rhythm section adapted to create a dynamic sound. I used music software to add body and fill in the gaps. I worked closely with each musician to ensure the arrangement fit their strengths, often staying after school to rehearse sections until the transitions were smooth.

Our first performance with the new arrangements drew positive feedback from both the audience and the band director. A visiting judge at a regional music festival commented on how creative the instrumentation sounded. More importantly, the band members felt confident and energized, knowing that the music had been shaped for them. My arrangements became a regular feature in our concerts, and other student musicians began asking for my help in adapting music for their ensembles. We even recorded our music and posted our novel sound on YouTube.

This experience reinforced my belief that a true skill can be a personal talent. However, sharing ideas broadly, provides the chance for others to insert their creativity. By learning to arrange music for our band, I discovered the satisfaction of blending creativity with collaboration. Whether I am working with musicians, classmates, or teammates, I approach each project with the same commitment to understand the strengths of the group, adapt the plan to fit those strengths, and create a result that everyone is proud to share.

Why This Works

- **Hook in Context**: Shows the problem that revealed the skill
- **Thesis**: Defines the talent in a clear, specific way
- **Detailed Development**: Shows learning and adaptation process
- **Real Impact**: Audience feedback and confidence boost
- **Reflection**: Links the skill to collaboration and future use

Brainstorming Questions

1. What is a skill you are known for among friends, teachers, or teammates?
2. How did you first discover this talent?
3. What steps did you take to improve it?
4. Who has benefited from your talent, and how?
5. Have you taught or shared this skill with others?
6. What challenges have you faced in developing it?
7. How will this skill be valuable in the future?

Skeleton Template

Paragraph 1: Hook, Context, Thesis - Describe the situation where you first recognized your talent or skill. End with a clear thesis statement about it.

Paragraph 2: Development - Show the steps you took to learn and improve the skill.

Paragraph 3: Impact - Give specific examples of how you used this skill and the results.

Paragraph 4: Reflection - Restate your thesis in new words and explain its importance in your life now and in the future.

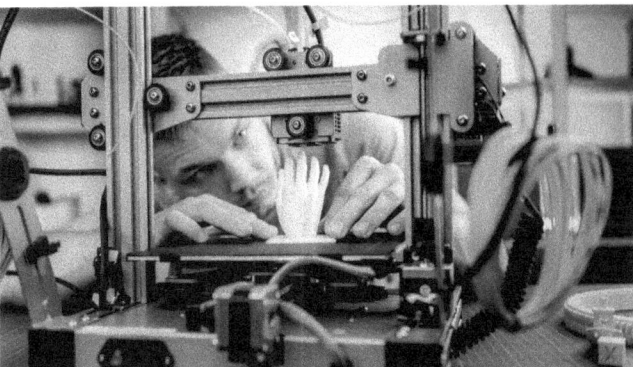

PIQ #4 – Educational Opportunity or Barrier Prompt:
Describe how you have taken advantage of a significant educational opportunity or worked to overcome an educational barrier.

UC's Real Goal - The University of California wants to know how you respond to obstacles or seize opportunities for growth. Strong responses show determination, planning, and a willingness to take action to ensure academic success, despite challenges or limitations.

Model Essay - 345 words

During my first year of high school, our Internet service was unreliable, often cutting out during evenings when I needed to research, write essays, or join online study sessions. I started going to the library and coffee shops where I sat for hours. Yet, I could not stay out too late, so I needed a better solution. The barrier became most challenging when our district shifted to remote learning. I realized that without a dependable solution, my academic performance and participation would suffer. I set a goal to create a personal system that allowed me to access learning materials consistently, even without stable Internet at home.

I began by speaking with my school librarian, who helped me borrow a mobile hotspot. I then mapped out public locations within walking distance that offered free Wi-Fi, such as the school's courtyard during lunch and a nearby café. I got my parents' permission to remain out later. To stay organized, I carried a portable charger and stored my files on a USB drive so I could work without missing anything. I scheduled specific times to use each location and built a routine that balanced study time with travel time.

The system worked. I maintained high grades, participated in group projects, and submitted every assignment on time. I even helped classmates who faced similar challenges by sharing my routine and teaching them how to use offline features on shared documents. By the end of the semester, I had developed a complete "mobile study hub" strategy that allowed me to work anywhere and stay connected to my teachers and peers.

This experience taught me that educational barriers can be overcome through planning, creativity, and resourcefulness. I found others to help me solve the problem. I, in turn, helped my classmates. By refusing to let unreliable Internet limit my learning, I developed problem-solving skills that continue to serve me in other areas. I now approach academic challenges with the same mindset: assess the resources available, design a strategy that works under the circumstances, and follow through until the goal is met.

Why This Works

- **Immediate Problem**: Starts with a specific, relatable barrier
- **Clear Goal**: Explains the exact objective in response to the barrier
- **Proactive Solutions**: Multiple concrete steps, not just one fix
- **Shared Benefit**: Helped others with the same challenge
- **Reflection**: Shows personal growth and adaptability

Brainstorming Questions

1. What is the most significant educational challenge you have faced?
2. What resources did you use to address it?
3. What strategies made your solution work?
4. Did you help others in the process?
5. What skills did you gain from this experience?
6. How did the challenge change your approach to learning?
7. How will this help you in future academic situations?

Skeleton Template

Paragraph 1: Hook, Context, Thesis - Describe the barrier or opportunity and your goal in addressing it.

Paragraph 2: Process - Outline the steps you took to work through the situation.

Paragraph 3: Results - Describe the measurable outcomes or changes.

Paragraph 4: Reflection - Restate your thesis in new words and explain how this shaped your approach to learning.

PIQ #5 – Significant Challenge Prompt: Describe the most significant challenge you have faced and the steps you have taken to overcome this challenge.

UC's Real Goal - The University of California is looking for evidence of resilience, responsibility, and problem-solving. They want to understand the steps you took, not just the difficulty you faced, and how you maintained or improved academic performance during the challenge.

Model Essay - 332 words

When my mother had surgery during my sophomore year, she needed several weeks of recovery at home. During that time, with my mom bedridden, I became the primary caregiver for my younger siblings, took care of the house, cooked meals, and kept up with schoolwork. Balancing my academic responsibilities with family support was the most demanding part of my high school experience. My goal became to manage household duties effectively without sacrificing my education.

I created a daily schedule that outlined times for preparing meals, helping my siblings with homework, and completing my own assignments. I created meal plans so we were not relying on unhealthy fast food deliveries. To make the workload manageable, I prepared simple meals in advance and set up a shared calendar so my siblings could see when I was available to help them with their homework. I also communicated openly with my teachers about my situation, which allowed me to adjust deadlines when absolutely necessary. This combination of structure and flexibility helped me meet my responsibilities on both fronts.

Although I was often exhausted, I noticed positive results. My siblings adjusted to a predictable routine, my mother's recovery progressed smoothly, and my grades remained strong. I worked harder to allocate time for sleep and set aside time for me to finish my own homework. Teachers expressed appreciation for my organization, communication, and commitment, while my mother frequently shared her gratitude, saying that my support allowed her to not worry so much about everything that needed to be done, but rather focus on healing. The experience built a stronger sense of trust and cooperation among everyone in my family.

This challenge taught me that perseverance is the result of discipline, not just determination. By creating a system, including everyone in my communication, and following a calendar with consistency, I learned how to balance competing priorities while meeting the needs of others. I now approach difficult situations with the understanding that preparation, communication, and flexibility are essential for success.

Why This Works

- **High-Stakes Situation**: Makes the challenge feel urgent and personal
- **Thesis States Goal**: Explains exactly what was at stake
- **Specific Actions**: Scheduling, meal prep, communication

- **Results**: Positive change for both family and academics
- **Reflection**: Links discipline and structure to perseverance

Brainstorming Questions

1. What is the most challenging personal or academic situation you have faced?
2. How did you plan your response?
3. What resources or people helped you?
4. What habits or strategies made the most difference?
5. How did the challenge affect your school performance?
6. What did you learn about yourself from this experience?
7. How will you use these skills in the future?

Skeleton Template

Paragraph 1: Hook, Context, Thesis - Describe the challenge and your goal in responding to the situations you faced. What impactful first sentence immediately tells the UC readers why this is so important to you? What thesis statement leads the reader into the rest of your story?

Paragraph 2: Actions - Explain the steps you took to address the challenge.

Paragraph 3: Results - Describe the improvements or changes that occurred.

Paragraph 4: Reflection - Restate your thesis and explain what you learned from the experience.

PIQ #6 – Favorite Academic Subject Prompt: Think about an academic subject that inspires you. Describe how you have furthered this interest inside and/or outside of the classroom.

UC's Real Goal - The University of California wants to see your intellectual curiosity and your ability to connect academic knowledge with real-world applications. They are looking for evidence that you actively deepen your learning beyond required coursework.

Model Essay - 340 words

Concepts in physics first captured my attention when I built a model roller coaster in my freshman year. The creative process of figuring out what I wanted, researching how on the Internet, and making the roller coaster track was a thrill. The mechanics of vehicle construction captivated my mind for hours. Then, watching the car speed down the track made me want to understand the forces at work. I realized that physics combines theory with real-world application, allowing ideas to move from equations on paper to tangible results. My goal became to explore this subject both in class and through hands-on projects.

I began by studying classical mechanics in greater depth, using online simulations to visualize concepts such as momentum and energy transfer. I applied this knowledge to design a skateboard ramp for my neighborhood park. By calculating angles, heights, and friction, I ensured that the ramp was both safe for the kids and challenging for those who were more experienced. Using an Excel spreadsheet, I recorded a data set I used for my calculations. I tracked performance data by timing runs and adjusting the structure to improve speed without sacrificing stability.

The project deepened my interest and demonstrated that physics can improve community spaces. Younger skateboarders appreciated the smoother surface and better balance, while experienced riders enjoyed the added speed. Parents and other community members applauded my efforts while city leaders complimented me in securing approvals for the construction. My teacher encouraged me to present my process and calculations at our school's science fair, where I explained the theoretical principles that guided every design decision I made along the way.

This experience reinforced my belief that physics is more than a school subject. I used the principles as a framework for understanding and improving the world around me. By applying classroom knowledge to a real project, I discovered the satisfaction of seeing abstract concepts produce practical benefits. I now approach both academic and personal challenges with a physics mindset to observe, analyze, and test until the best solution emerges.

Why This Works

- **Hook with Discovery**: Shows curiosity sparked by a project
- **Thesis**: Connects passion to goal
- **Application**: Links classroom learning to real-world design

- **Community Impact**: Benefits others through the subject
- **Reflection**: Defines mindset gained from subject

Brainstorming Questions

1. Which subject excites you the most and why?
2. What projects or activities have you done in that subject outside class?
3. How have you deepened your knowledge?
4. Has your work in this subject helped others?
5. What skills have you gained from studying it?
6. How does this subject connect to your future goals?
7. How do you approach challenges in this subject?

Skeleton Template

Paragraph 1: Hook, Context, Thesis - Describe how you became interested in the subject and your goal in exploring it.

Paragraph 2: Actions - Explain how you pursued your interest through learning and projects.

Paragraph 3: Results - Show how your work benefited others or led to new opportunities.

Paragraph 4: Reflection - Restate your thesis and connect the subject to your future approach to learning.

PIQ #7 – Making Your School or Community Better Prompt:
What have you done to make your school or your community a better place?

UC's Real Goal - The University of California wants to see how you identify needs in your community and take initiative to address them. They are looking for concrete actions, measurable results, and an understanding of how those changes impact others.

Model Essay - 346 words

I noticed classmates struggling to complete homework. A few students explained that they lacked quiet study spaces at home. Some said they needed help with their assignments. Still others said they felt more motivated when there were others studying at the same time. I decided to figure out a way to make studying cool and accessible for anyone who wanted to participate. Starting small, I began by setting up a table in the cafeteria during lunch where students could work together and create a welcoming space that encouraged academic support and collaboration.

At first, only a few friends joined me, but as word spread, more students stopped by for help from our friendly, inclusive group. I organized more tables, but this time organized by subject, inviting volunteers from honor societies to assist with math, science, writing, and Spanish. To make the space more appealing, I brought extra pencils and paper. I even purchased stickers for people to use as they liked when they succeeded. Over time, the "Homework Help Tables" grew into a recognized tutoring club with regular volunteers and a schedule posted in the cafeteria.

Students commented that they felt more confident about their schoolwork, and teachers noticed improvements in students' work, especially with those who often did not turn in their homework assignments. The students started doing significantly better on their quizzes and tests, too. The principal praised the program and offered to pay for resources and supplies. One day, he even bought everyone lunch. By the end of the year, our club had assisted dozens of students and created a stronger sense of peer support within the school.

This experience showed me that improving a community begins with identifying a need and taking consistent action to address the problem, growing one step at a time. By starting with a single table and building the project into a school-wide resource, I learned that meaningful change often begins small and can grow as large as the group wants with consistent effort. I now look for ways to strengthen connections and resources wherever I am involved.

Why This Works

- **Identifies a Need**: Clear reason for taking action
- **Thesis in First Paragraph**: States the improvement goal
- **Growth Over Time**: Shows small beginnings to large impact

- **Results**: Concrete changes in school performance and support
- **Reflection**: Connects lesson to future approach to leadership

Brainstorming Questions

1. What problem did you notice in your school or community?
2. What first step did you take to address it?
3. Who helped you or joined your effort?
4. How did your project grow or change over time?
5. What results did you see?
6. How did others react to your work?
7. What did you learn about improving communities?

Skeleton Template

Paragraph 1: Hook, Context, Thesis - Describe the activity and your commitment to service and the community. Maybe you witnessed a serious issue. How did you fix the problem? Consider food banks and poverty, kids needing a coach, trees planted on barren land, fish trapped in nets, the elderly needing companionship, support for domestic violence victims, awareness project related to guns, drugs, gangs, or bullying, or maybe cleanup projects at parks, beaches, and recreation centers.

Paragraph 2: Actions - Explain the steps you took to begin and grow your project.

Paragraph 3: Results - Describe the changes and outcomes in your school or community.

Paragraph 4: Reflection - Restate your thesis and explain what you learned about making change.

PIQ #8 – Something Else Prompt: Beyond what you have already shared, what makes you stand out as a strong candidate for admission to the University of California?

UC's Real Goal - The University of California wants to know about a unique quality, passion, or project that reveals something important about you. This is a chance to share a meaningful story that has not fit elsewhere but shows your initiative, creativity, and contribution.

Model Essay (336 words)

On the weekends, I restore old bicycles and donate them to children in my neighborhood. I started this project after noticing several unused, broken bikes sitting in garages and on the curbs. Growing up, I constantly fixed up my bike, upgrading the tires and brakes while also giving my only means of transportation a spiffed-up paint job. My passion for bikes led me on a three-year journey to find as many discarded bikes as possible, repairing them so they could be enjoyed again by local kids.

At first, I learned repair techniques from online tutorials and a local bike shop, focusing on cleaning chains, fixing brakes, and replacing worn tires. My skills continued to improve as I communicated with online hobbyists who shared their creative strategies. By putting out requests, I collected donated bikes from neighbors and salvaged parts from unrepairable models. After each restoration, I delivered the bicycle to a child who needed one, often adjusting the seat and handlebars on the spot to fit the rider.

Over the past three years, the demand has grown. Needing to expand my reach, I began hunting for bicycles in dumpsters and junkyards, often finding unexpected items I could also repair. Still, I remained focused on locating unwanted, neglected, and abandoned bicycles, waiting for me to find. Thus far, I have repaired more than fifty bicycles, turning my hobby into a part-time business, which has enabled me to buy new parts and supplies.

Parents often tell me how much their children enjoy riding to the park or school. The local community center invited me to lead a bike repair workshop, giving me a chance to teach others the skills I had developed. This project affirmed my belief that making a difference can be as simple as recognizing potential where others see waste. By giving old bicycles a second life, I provided children with freedom, exercise, and joy. I now approach opportunities with the mindset that value can be created through creativity, effort, and a willingness to share skills.

Why This Works

- **Unique Topic**: Uncommon project stands out immediately
- **Clear Goal**: Defined from the beginning
- **Community Benefit**: Measurable and personal impact
- **Growth**: From personal project to community teaching
- **Reflection**: Connects to a broader life philosophy

Brainstorming Questions

1. What activity or passion is central to your identity?
2. How did you begin and why?
3. What challenges did you overcome to pursue it?
4. Who benefited from your work?
5. How did it grow or expand over time?
6. What lessons did you learn?
7. How does this reflect your character and goals?

Skeleton Template

Paragraph 1: Hook, Context, Thesis - Introduce your unique quality or project and your goal.

Paragraph 2: Actions - Describe the steps you took and the skills you developed.

Paragraph 3: Results - Explain the impact on others and yourself.

Paragraph 4: Reflection - Restate your thesis and connect the experience to your future.

Chapter 9:
Warning - AI, Authenticity, & Verification

The University of California's warning to applicants who use AI or provide inaccurate or false information

I. Introduction

In the age of artificial intelligence, college applicants face a new frontier. AI, essay-writing tools, and editing software offer powerful advantages, but they also raise ethical concerns. The University of California, like many other schools, has issued explicit warnings about the use of AI and the importance of authenticity in application materials. This chapter explores the University of California's policies and how students can avoid jeopardizing their applications.

II. UC's Official Policy on AI and Misrepresentation

According to the UC Application Guide:

> "Providing false or misleading information, including using AI-generated content or material written by others, may result in cancellation of your application, admission revocation, or disciplinary action."

UC's warning is direct and unambiguous. Whether through a ghostwriter, generative AI, or factual fabrication, submitting inauthentic materials is a violation of the university's Code of Conduct. Applicants must understand that any attempt to mislead, even with good intentions, undermines the admissions process.

III. What Counts as "False or Misleading"

Misrepresentation goes beyond academic dishonesty. It includes:

- **Falsifying Accomplishments:** Listing internships or awards not actually earned.
- **Inflating Roles:** Claiming to be "president" of a club when one was a general member.
- **Inaccurate Hours:** Logging exaggerated community service or work hours.
- **AI-Written Essays:** Submitting ChatGPT-generated essays is ethically wrong.

Anecdote: The admission of an Orange County high school senior was rescinded from a top UC after a club advisor reported that the student had misrepresented his leadership roles. During verification, the UC learned that the student was never the co-founder and president, roles he previously claimed.

IV. The Ethics of AI Use in College Applications

AI is not inherently unethical. However, misuse occurs when students let AI substitute for their writing.

Consider the difference:

- **Ethical Use:** "I used Grammarly and ChatGPT to help brainstorm word choices for my PIQ response. I rewrote the PIQ first and used AI as a personal thesaurus."
- **Unethical Use:** "I typed the PIQ prompt with my personal information into ChatGPT and submitted what AI generated. I then read and edited the result."

UC admissions officers read thousands of essays. They can recognize generic, over-polished content. An authentic story with imperfect grammar often reads stronger than an AI-generated masterpiece lacking soul. Besides, AI-generated essays read in an unnatural way, often using strangely placed words.

V. Real-World Implications & Enforcement

The UC system has tools to detect fraud:

- Plagiarism detection software (e.g., Turnitin or similar tools)
- Internal comparisons between writing samples and standardized test essays
- Manual review by admissions readers trained to spot AI-generated language patterns

Anecdote: In 2023, a Northern California applicant submitted essays with suspicious phrasing. A follow-up phone interview with pointed questions revealed that the student could not elaborate. Their admission was rescinded. *Note:* Some students cannot even define or describe the words they used in their essays.

VI. Verifying the Truth: The Application Audit Process

UC conducts random and cause-based audits:

- Contacting references listed in activity sections
- Requesting documentation for honors or research
- Interviewing students to verify written statements

This is why it helps to keep a log or folder with:

- Supervisor names and contact information (Start early since it is often much harder later.)
- Screenshots of awards, letters, or certificates (Sometimes these get misplaced; take pictures.)
- Project timelines and deliverables (What did you do? How? When? Where? With whom?)

Anecdote: A student applying to UC Davis included a robotics competition in their activities. During a verification audit, they were able to produce a photo of the competition, their name on the team roster, and a link to a press release validating their claims.

VII. Best Practices for Staying Ethical and Authentic

- **Document Everything:** Use a spreadsheet or journal.
- **Work Offline First:** Draft essays by hand or in a digital document.
- **Get Feedback Wisely:** Ask trusted mentors who know you, not strangers or anonymous editors.

- **Use AI Cautiously:** Not as a ghostwriter.

Reflection activity: Highlight three experiences in your Activities & Awards section. For each, ask yourself: Could I provide evidence or articulate the details if I were asked to have an interview?

VIII. Reflection Questions and Self-Audit

- Did I write this essay myself, using my voice and insights?
- Could I explain every activity or accomplishment listed?
- If asked to verify or explain something tomorrow, would I be prepared?

These are not just questions for admissions, but for personal integrity. Your story, told honestly, will always be more compelling than one told by AI.

IX. Conclusion

AI is a powerful, but it cannot substitute your voice, your truth, or your integrity. The University of California wants to admit real students with real stories, not perfect essays written by an algorithm. As technology advances, so will verification methods. But what remains timeless is authenticity.

Use the application as a mirror, not a mask. Who you are is good enough.

Chapter 10:
The PIQ Workbook

Brainstorming and crafting standout UC Personal Insight Questions

You have read my suggestions, reviewed samples, learned why it works and now you need to start writing...if you have not started before. Create the arc in your story.

Remember that your PIQs are not about proving that you are perfect. They are designed to get to know you and prove you are real, thoughtful, and ready to bring something unique to a UC campus. Your stories matter. Tell them with honesty and detail, and you will give the admissions team a reason to picture you there next fall.

hook → context → action → reflection

PIQ Writing Flow

1. **Pick the Prompt** → Match a story that shows a *different side of you*.
2. **Hook** → Start mid-action or with a vivid image.
3. **Context** → Who, what, where, why it mattered.
4. **Action** → Specific steps you took.
5. **Reflection** → Growth, insight, connection to your future.

The PIQ Reference & Quick Checklist

Prompt #	Core Quality	Quick Story Ideas
1	Leadership	Club officer, leading a project, resolving a team conflict
2	Creativity	DIY solutions, art/music/dance, inventing something
3	Talent/Skill	Repairing, coding, mentoring, athletic skill
4	Opportunity/Barrier	Language learning, special program, lack of resources
5	Challenge	Injury, family change, academic struggle
6	Favorite Subject	Class project, competition, independent research
7	Community Betterment	Fundraiser, clean-up, tutoring others
8	Something Else	Personal tradition, unique hobby, cultural connection

PIQ #1 – Leadership Experience Prompt: Describe an example of your leadership experience in which you have positively influenced others, helped resolve disputes, or contributed to group efforts over time.

UC's Real Goal: They want to see how you act in moments that require responsibility, vision, or problem-solving. A title is not necessary.

Brainstorm Prompts:

- A time you stepped up when no one else would
- A group conflict you helped resolve
- A time you led without having an official role
- A situation where the leader did not show up and you needed to take charge
- An initiative you started or improved
- A moment you realized your leadership style

Skeleton Template:

"[Group or team] was struggling with [specific problem]. Tension rose because [brief detail about the conflict or challenge].
As [your role], I [specific action you took].
[Describe how you involved others or encouraged collaboration].
In the end, [specific measurable result] and [emotional/relational result].
Leadership, I learned [surface-level symbol of leadership] and more about [your personal insight]."

Your Draft Here:

_____

_____

_____

_____

_____

_____

_____

_____

PIQ #2 – Creativity Prompt: Every person has a creative side, and it can be expressed in many ways. Describe how you express your creative side.

UC's Real Goal: They want to see how you think outside the box and create original solutions, projects, or expressions.

Brainstorm Prompts:

- A time you solved a problem in an unexpected way
- A project where you used unconventional materials or methods
- A way you blend different interests into something new
- A mathematical, science, robotics, rocket, or other problem that required creativity
- A time you expressed yourself through art, music, writing, or another medium
- Pride in an invention or design

Skeleton Template:

"When [specific challenge] happened, I had to get creative. I turned to [unconventional source of materials/ ideas].
[Describe two or three vivid, specific transformations you made].
[Moment of success, recognition, or reaction from others].
I realized that creativity is not [common assumption], but [your personal definition of creativity]."

Your Draft Here:

_____

_____

_____

_____

_____

_____

_____

_____

_____

_____

_____

PIQ #3 – Greatest Talent or Skill Prompt: What would you say is your greatest talent or skill? How have you developed and demonstrated that talent over time?

UC's Real Goal: They want to see dedication, perseverance, and an area you focused on or cultivated. The talent may be a skill, ability, or some talent you cultivated and shared.

Brainstorm Prompts:

- A skill you practiced over time until you became great
- A talent you used to help others or create something valuable
- A time you improved this skill despite challenges
- How you first discovered your ability
- What people often come to you for help - math, science, mechanics
- Athletic or artistic talents developed over time

Skeleton Template:

"I've always had a knack for [specific skill]. My first attempt was [brief, vivid description of early version].
Over time, I grew this skill by [specific actions you took to improve].
Now, I [describe current, more advanced application of the skill].
It started as [simple motivation], but became [deeper purpose or community impact].
Every time I [repeat the skill in action], I am reminded that [core insight about persistence, problem-solving, or growth]."

Your Draft Here:

_____

_____

_____

_____

_____

_____

_____

_____

_____

_____

_____

_____

PIQ #4 – Educational Opportunity or Barrier Prompt: Describe how you have taken advantage of a significant educational opportunity or worked to overcome an educational barrier.

UC's Real Goal: They want to see how you turn challenges into opportunities or make the most of unique chances to grow.

Brainstorm Prompts:

- A program, class, or mentor who gave you new opportunities
- A barrier like language, finances, resources, or location you had to overcome
- A time you pushed yourself beyond what was expected academically
- A turning point in your education that shaped you
- A time you made your own learning opportunities
- You took part in COSMOS, research, contests, or competitions

Skeleton Template:

"When [specific barrier or opportunity] appeared, I [initial reaction].
At first, [describe early challenges or hesitations].
Then, [explain turning point and what you did to engage or overcome].
Over time, I [describe growth and specific success].
This taught me that [lesson about resilience, connection, or opportunity]."

Your Draft Here:

_____

_____

_____

_____

_____

_____

_____

_____

_____

_____

PIQ #5 – Significant Challenge Prompt: Describe the most significant challenge you have faced and the steps you have taken to overcome this challenge.

UC's Real Goal: They want to see resilience and how you handle setbacks to keep going.

Brainstorm Prompts:

- A personal event or injury that shaped your character
- A family challenge death or disruption that led to chaos and reflection
- A physical, emotional, or academic setback you overcame
- A time you had to rebuild yourself after a loss
- The hardest decision you have ever made
- A challenge that forced you to grow faster than expected

Skeleton Template:

"In [specific time period], I faced [describe the challenge briefly but vividly].
Losing [activity, opportunity, or ability] felt like [emotional impact].
I started [describe small steps you took toward improvement or adaptation].
Along the way, I [learned something unexpected or gained a new skill].
By the end, I understood that [shifted perspective about strength, success, or self-worth]."

Your Draft Here:

_____

_____

_____

_____

_____

_____

_____

_____

_____

_____

_____

PIQ #6 – Favorite Academic Subject Prompt: Think about an academic subject that inspires you. Describe how you have furthered this interest inside and/or outside of the classroom.

UC's Real Goal: They want to see your intellectual curiosity and how you take learning beyond class requirements.

Brainstorm Prompts:

- A specific topic within your favorite subject that excites you
- A project, experiment, or research you pursued on your own
- A way you connect your favorite subject to real-world action
- How this subject ties into your future goals
- A moment you realized your passion for the subject
- A class, teacher, collaboration, or project that shaped your interest

Skeleton Template:

"[Subject] is more than [common stereotype about the subject]; it is [your unique take].
After learning about [specific topic or concept], I [describe how you explored it further outside class].
I [describe concrete project, research, or application].
[Describe recognition, impact, or next steps].
This subject drives me because [personal connection or future goal]."

Your Draft Here:

_____

_____

_____

_____

_____

_____

_____

_____

_____

_____

PIQ #7 – Making Your School or Community Better Prompt:
What have you done to make your school or your community a better place?

UC's Real Goal: They want to see initiative, impact, and personal investment in your environment.

Brainstorm Prompts:

- A problem you noticed and decided to fix
- A group you supported or organized
- A time you created something that improved life for others
- A moment you realized you could create real change
- A visible result of your efforts

Skeleton Template:

"When I saw [specific issue in your school/community], I decided to act.
I [list two or three concrete steps you took to make change].
[Describe a moment during the process that felt meaningful or showed community involvement].
Now, [describe the lasting result or visible change].
This taught me that [personal belief about impact, responsibility, or change]."

Your Draft Here:

_____

_____

_____

_____

_____

_____

_____

_____

_____

_____

_____

PIQ #8 – Something Else Prompt: Beyond what you have already shared, what makes you stand out as a strong candidate for admission to the University of California?

UC's Real Goal: They want to see uniqueness or some meaningful aspect of your life, family, beliefs, or vision they would not learn anywhere else in your application.

Brainstorm Prompts:

- A tradition or hobby that reflects your values
- A personal story that shows your character or worldview
- A way you connect different parts of your identity
- A passion that shapes your daily life
- A project or habit that reflects your goals
- A family value, belief, or travel experience
- An everyday act you take for granted but that taught you lessons

Skeleton Template:

"Every [specific tradition, habit, or unique activity], I [describe action using sensory details].
To me, [redefine or deepen the meaning of this tradition/habit].
That's why I [describe specific action, project, or creation that comes from it].
I [connect your activity/quality to a broader theme, like bridging cultures, leading change, or connecting people]."

Your Draft Here:

_____

_____

_____

_____

_____

_____

_____

_____

_____

_____

_____

_____

Lizard Publishing creates, designs, produces, and distributes books and resources to provide academic, admissions, and career information. Our mental process is fueled by three tenets:

- Ignite the hunger to learn and the passion to make a difference
- Illuminate the expanse of knowledge by sharing cutting-edge thinking
- Innovate to create a world that makes the transition from dreams to reality

We work with academic leaders who transform the educational landscape to publish relevant content and advise students of their educational and professional options, with the aim of developing 21st-century learners and leaders. We also work with students to publish their books and present widely diverse ideas to the college/graduate school-bound community. With headquarters in Irvine, California, Lizard Publishing works virtually with authors to edit, publish, and distribute both hard copy and paperback books.

Below are a few of our books that you might find extremely valuable. These are available on Amazon.

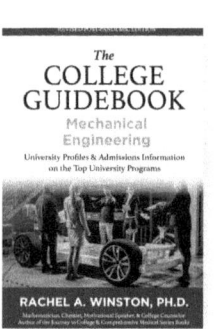
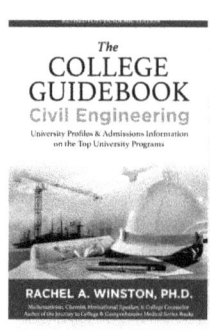
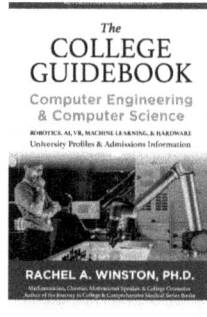

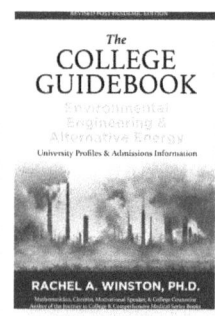